"Doug Giles is a good man, and his bambinas are fearless. His girls Hannah and Regis Giles are indefatigable. I admire the Giles clan from afar."

— Dennis Miller

"Doug Giles must be some kind of a great guy if CNN wants to impugn him."

— Rush Limbaugh

"Doug Giles is a substantive and funny force for traditional values."

— Ann Coulter

"Doug Giles speaks the truth - he's a societal watchdog - a funny bastard."

— Ted Nugent

My Grandpa is a Patriotic Badass!

Doug Giles

Copyright 2017, Doug Giles, All Rights Reserved

No part of this book may be reproduced, stored in a retrieval system, or transmitted by any means without the written permission of the author.

Published by White Feather Press. (www.whitefeatherpress.com)

ISBN 978-1-61808-160-5

Printed in the United States of America

Cover design by David Bugnon

Cover and meme photo by FPG/Hulton Archive/Getty Images

White Feather Press

Reaffirming Faith in God, Family, and Country!

Dedication

This punchy book is dedicated to all the hard-core, patriotic, grandfathers out there who are preserving our freedoms, their families and our flag. I'd like to thank you and salute you. And please, for the love of God and Country, stay vocal, stay active, instruct your grandkids well, cherish this grand experiment in self-governance, and, of course, always stay rowdy.

Doug Giles
Somewhere in Texas
October 2017

Other books by Doug Giles

Pussification: The Effeminization of the American Male

Raising Righteous and Rowdy Girls

Raising Boys Feminists Will Hate

Ruling in Babylon: Seven Habits of Highly Effective Twentysomethings

Political Twerps, Cultural Jerks, Church Quirks

The Bulldog Attitude: Get It or Get Left Behind

10 Habits of Decidedly Defective People: The Successful Loser's Guide to Life

A Time to Clash: Papers from a Provocative Pastor

If You're Going Through Hell, Keep Going

Preface

How do you want your grandkids to remember you?

Would you like them to remember you as a paunched-gut, passive, non-involved, checked-out and indolent dolt? No? I'm with you on that one, buddy. Doesn't sound too sexy, eh?

I want my grandkids to remember me as a Patriotic Badass!

Sure, I want them to remember me as a loving and doting, wise and funny, handsome and articulate, hunter and angler, oil painter and Christ-following super-hero, but primarily ... I'd like to be known as a Patriotic Badass.

That's why I compiled the most viral and quotable, pro-America one-liners, that I've ever penned.

The following quotes have spawned memes and columns that have accounted for a big chunk of the 213 Million page views on my website, ClashDaily.com.

These maxims have also fomented some of the most hilarious hatred from the ubiquitous liberal snowflakes and I love it.

"Secretly, everybody's getting tired of political correctness, kissing up. That's the kiss-ass generation we're in right now. We're really in a pussy generation."

- Clint Eastwood

Hi. My name is Hamish. My grandpa is my buddy. He likes to hunt and fish with me. He also likes to draw with me and tell me funny stories about what he did when he was little.

My grandpa also really likes God a lot, our family and America. He talks about them all the time. He says some people don't like him talking about God and politics. He calls them 'liberals.' I don't know what that is but I don't think it is good.

My grandpa also doesn't like TV too much or this town called Hollywood. I've never been to this Hollywood place but my grandpa says, it sucks and that's why we live in the Republic of Texas. He really likes Texas. He says, Texas is like a cold glass of lemonade with two shots of Tequila and ten tablespoons of attitude.

Here's some other things my grandpa says. Does your grandpa say stuff like this?

My Grandpa Says ...

"Rebellion to tyrants is obedience to God, and if you're gonna get a tattoo then tattoo that phrase on your arm in big, bold letters."

My Grandpa Says ...

"He thanks Jesus
every day that
some lady he calls,
The Hildebeest,
didn't get elected
President."

My Grandpa Says …

"If you don't like our Constitution, The Bill of Rights or The Declaration of Independence, then you can kiss his freedom-loving ass! My grandma doesn't like him saying that in front of me but she smiles anyway and agrees with him."

My Grandpa Says ...

"If women want to march, they should march over to his house and fix him a sandwich and get him a beer!"

My Grandpa Says ...

"Everyone should be treated kindly until they act like an idiot. He believes everyone is created in God's image and should be given respect until that person acts like some lady named ... Kathy Griffin."

My Grandpa Says ...

"Political Correctness is a mode of speech that is often employed when one is trying not to offend a whiny pussy."

My Grandpa Says ...

"If Liberals and The NFL wish to be known as, 'The people who protest our flag and our National Anthem,' I say let them. Let them ride that crap-train straight into a self-destructive political ditch."

My Grandpa Says ...

"Socialism is like a nude beach: It sounds great until you actually see it."

My Grandpa Says ...

"If they make a movie about Obama, what woman should Hollywood choose to play Barack?"

My Grandpa Says ...

"CNN is to news what Nancy Pelosi is to MENSA and pole dancing."

My Grandpa Says ...

"Maxine Waters is nuttier than a squirrel turd."

My Grandpa Says ...

"Michael Moore and Rosie O'Donnell should get married and move to STFU Island."

My Grandpa Says …

"He completely understands why Bill cheated on Hillary, and he empathizes with Bubba's plight."

My Grandpa Says ...

"Little kids should play with toy guns and be trained at an early age to fight against terrorists and liberal anarchists who physically harm law-abiding citizens."

My Grandpa Says ...

"Leftists and Islam need people to be cowardly, docile and house-trained."

My Grandpa Says ...

"Liberals must eradicate a man's masculinity in order for their evil machinations to thrive; and they're doing a good job of making males spineless weasels aplenty ... a society of frightened men."

My Grandpa Says ...

"He agrees with Clint Eastwood; this generation is a pussy generation."

My Grandpa Says ...

"He trusts politicians about as far as he can throw a big fat strudel-hun who's holding a Ford F150's rear axle."

My Grandpa Says ...

"His liberty is a right given to him by God and not some gift given to him by Chucky Schumer."

My Grandpa Says ...

"There are three ugly truths that keep him from being a democrat:

1). Debbie.
2). Wasserman.
3). Schultz."

My Grandpa Says ...

"If he had to choose between marrying Debbie Wasserman Schultz and Ricky Martin, he'd have to go with Mr. Martin."

My Grandpa Says ...

"He prefers his way of doing things over your way of not doing them."

My Grandpa Says ...

"Rebellion is good and a necessary tool to ward off big-government tools and that good parents should teach their kids how to perfect the middle finger against tyrants."

My Grandpa Says ...

"America's needs should come first and screw everyone else until we're back in great shape. #MAGA!"

My Grandpa Says ...

"He's so happy he doesn't have to listen to Michelle Obama's angry, control freak, crap anymore."

My Grandpa Says ...

"Never ask a lady if she's pregnant unless you see a baby popping out of her the very moment you ask."

My Grandpa Says ...

"We should call the man-bun a douche-knot."

My Grandpa Says ...

"If a gay couple wants a gay wedding cake then they should go to a frickin' gay cake maker. Either that or, buy some Betty Crocker cake mix and bake your own damn cake and quit throwing a fit about cakes because ... It's so gay."

My Grandpa Says ...

"If you're going to be gay at least be a man about it."

My Grandpa Says ...

"He's not homophobic ... he's ... Chick-O-Centric."

My Grandpa Says ...

"If lesbians hate men
so much, then why do
a lot of them end up
looking like
John Goodman?"

My Grandpa Says …

"Bruce Jenner will always be a dude no matter how big his implants get."

My Grandpa Says ...

"We shouldn't call gender-confused people derogatory names. We should be kind like Jesus, and simply refer to them as 'Men who talk too much.'"

My Grandpa Says ...

"If the sight of Vaseline turns you on, you've been living alone in your mom's basement for far too long."

My Grandpa Says ...

"PUSSIFICATION: The Effeminization Of The American Male, is one of the most important books of The 21st Century."

My Grandpa Says …

"If Muslims build a Mosque next door to his house, then he's going to take up pig farming and only hire beautiful girls who wear Daisy Dukes."

My Grandpa Says ...

"If Muslims don't like his beer drinking or our national Anthem, then they can pack their junk and move back to Suckistan."

My Grandpa Says …

"Europe made a big mistake welcoming Islamic immigrants."

My Grandpa Says ...

"Europe is toast; they'll never recover from the Islamic invasion, and forty years from now they'll be Islam's prison chick. Mop head wig and all, girlfriend."

My Grandpa Says ...

"If Obama ever made it on to our nation's currency it should be for a new denomination called, The Zero Dollar Bill."

My Grandpa Says ...

"Never trust someone who's never been punched in the face."

My Grandpa Says …

"Never trust obese people who smoke cigarettes."

My Grandpa Says ...

"Never take a laxative and a big shot of NyQuil just before going to bed."

My Grandpa Says ...

"If a guy wants to manscape, to never do it with a straight razor."

My Grandpa Says ...

"If me and my friends decide to jump ramps over people, be the dude on the bike."

My Grandpa Says ...

"People should be humble and not talk about how great or smart they are or how much money they have. He says, the most important things are family, character, integrity and humility. Everything else is donkey dung."

My Grandpa Says ...

"He prefers bacon,
beer and bikinis over
Sharia Law."

My Grandpa Says ...

"Kids should call older men 'sir' and older women 'ma'am' and not call them by their first name until they ask you to. He also says, good kids say, Mr, Mrs. and Miss to older people until the person says it's okay not to."

My Grandpa Says ...

"Good boys open doors for women and children."

My Grandpa Says ...

"Kids should help around the house and not be lazy and mouthy, ungrateful, little bastards."

My Grandpa Says ...

"Kids should learn how to say please and thank you when they're real little. He says that keeps them from being self-obsessed-me-monkeys when they get older."

My Grandpa Says ...

"We're in big trouble because Islamic young men love death and American young males love Frappuccinos."

My Grandpa Says ...

"Hillary Clinton deserves a gold medal for her ability to sling bullshit."

My Grandpa Says ...

"Journalism died kissing Hillary's butt, without taking a breath, in 2016."

My Grandpa Says ...

"Crooked Hillary is the perfect nickname for that old lardy hagfish."

My Grandpa Says ...

"It's not okay for some rancid, sexually confused, drag queen, to use the women's bathroom next to nine-year-old little girls."

My Grandpa Says ...

"If Trump is 'so evil' then why are his kids so amazing?"

My Grandpa Says ...

"A Christian can be a Christian, or a liberal, but he can't be both."

My Grandpa Says ...

"The U.S. should leave the U.N. and Trump should turn The U.N. headquarters in New York City into condos."

My Grandpa Says ...

"We shouldn't let people into America who want to kill us. Duh."

My Grandpa Says ...

"Welfare brats, who defraud taxpayers, should go to prison."

My Grandpa Says ...

Able-bodied welfare recipients are a stain on what it means to be a human."

My Grandpa Says ...

"It's weird that liberals hate Trump more than radical Islam and communist dictators."

My Grandpa Says ...

"Gays should be more concerned about Islam than Christians, because Islam will kill them and Christians will only pray for them, buy them a TobyMac album and maybe invite them to a Mike Huckabee conference."

My Grandpa Says ...

"The Left would lose very badly if they started a civil war with liberty-minded, 2nd Amendment folks."

My Grandpa Says ...

"The Media (D) lies more often than Rosie hits The Golden Corral Buffet line during her 5pm feeding."

My Grandpa Says ...

"If the founding of The United States were up to today's liberals, it would be called, The United States of Pussification."

My Grandpa Says ...

"If you hire lazy and entitled, grievance mongers, then bend over now and kiss your businesses' butt good-bye."

My Grandpa Says ...

"If you have to show an ID to coach little league, you should have to present an ID in order to vote."

My Grandpa Says ...

"The Bro Romper, Brotox and Diet Whiskey are probably the dumbest things that have been invented in recent years, and if you use any of the aforementioned, then please don't friend request him on Facebook."

My Grandpa Says ...

"A mixed drink is whiskey with ice."

My Grandpa Says …

"Smoking cigars is a sin only if you smoke one that's below a 90 rating in Cigar Aficionado."

My Grandpa Says …

"He agrees with President Trump that Rosie O'Donnell is a disgusting pig."

My Grandpa Says ...

"He'd rather milk a wolverine than slow dance with Nancy Pelosi."

My Grandpa Says ...

"Obama wasn't an incompetent President ... he intentionally weakened America's economy, divided our nation, depleted our international prowess and wrecked our military."

My Grandpa Says ...

"Obama was the worst president we have ever had."

My Grandpa Says ...

"Just because you're offended, it doesn't mean you're right."

My Grandpa Says ...

"If you're a male and still living with your mommy and you're 28 years old, then you should buy a sledgehammer and hit yourself in the face with it."

My Grandpa Says ...

"A good woman should avoid a spineless man."

My Grandpa Says ...

"Mammas don't let your babies grow up to be liberals."

My Grandpa Says ...

"If you want to raise awesome kids, then keep them away from public schools, Hollywood and effeminate branches of evangelicalism."

My Grandpa Says ...

"His middle finger is gluten free."

My Grandpa Says ...

"If you pay six bucks for Starbucks coffee, then you're a special kind of stupid."

My Grandpa Says ...

"If you want to better yourself, get rid of all your dumb ass friends and hang out with people who are better than you."

My Grandpa Says ...

"If you're around accomplished people, you should listen more than you talk, because they trump you."

My Grandpa Says ...

"Only pathetic losers blame other people for their mistakes. If you blow it ... then own it. Don't be like Obama who blamed Bush, Fox News and Rush for 'why' he was such an abysmal failure. Be a man, and take responsibility!"

My Grandpa Says ...

"Just because you're a christian, it doesn't mean you have to be a pussy."

My Grandpa Says ...

"Christians who don't positively impact politics and culture are worthless. If you think that's too harsh ... he says to read Matthew 5:13."

My Grandpa Says ...

"If Christians don't labor to implement a biblical worldview in all spheres of society, then they shouldn't complain when our culture goes to hell."

My Grandpa Says ...

"Guns have only two enemies rust and politicians."

My Grandpa Says ...

"Perfect the martial art of jiu jitsu and become proficient in shooting guns because of all the violent liberals out there."

My Grandpa Says ...

"Never let someone, or something that threatens you get in your personal space."

My Grandpa Says ...

"Never say, I've got a gun. If you need to use deadly force, the first sound they hear should be ... Boom!"

My Grandpa Says ...

"The average response time of a 911 call is 20 minutes; the response time of his three-fifty-seven magnum is 1200 feet per second."

My Grandpa Says ...

"Gun-free zones are a mass murderer's wet dream."

My Grandpa Says ...

"Teachers should pack heat in case students are attacked."

My Grandpa Says ...

"The first rule in a gunfight is to bring a gun, and the second rule is to win."

My Grandpa Says ...

"Make your attacker advance through a wall of bullets"

My Grandpa Says ...

"Never start a fight, but if someone else does, open up a 64-ounce can of whup ass on them."

My Grandpa Says ...

"Gun control is putting the second round into the hole the first bullet created."

My Grandpa Says ...

"That flag burners should all move to Iran and try that crap over there."

My Grandpa Says ...

"Liberals hate home schooling because they can't directly brainwash your kids for eight hours a day."

My Grandpa Says ...

"Universities have officially become ... The Liberals' Madrasas."

My Grandpa Says ...

"If you don't work
... you don't eat. He
said some guy named,
The Apostle Paul,
agrees with him."

My Grandpa Says ...

"Undertake something that's tough ... you'll be all the better for it."

My Grandpa Says ...

"You should have a clear-cut vision with the tenacity to see it fulfilled."

My Grandpa Says ...

"Always work your butt off. Hard and smart work is righteous stuff."

My Grandpa Says ...

"Get away from negative people. Even if they're 'family.' Jesus did."

My Grandpa Says ...

"Self-reliance and independence beats being a codependent wage slave."

My Grandpa Says ...

"You should feel bad if you're wasting time."

My Grandpa Says ...

"Winners are impervious
to the criticisms
of envious dorks."

My Grandpa Says ...

"Complainers suck the life out of relationships and end up living in a van down by the river."

My Grandpa Says ...

"Boldly face your fears with faith and always move forward."

My Grandpa Says ...

"Never feel self-pity ... pick yourself up, dust yourself off and ... keep kicking ass!"

My Grandpa Says ...

"If you're going through hell ... keep going."

My Grandpa Says ...

"Envy is the only sin that people will never confess and never enjoy."

My Grandpa Says ...

"Avoid being overly cautious and negative."

My Grandpa Says ...

"Excuse makers are self-deceived and deceiving."

My Grandpa Says ...

"If you build your life on God's word you can stand this life's BS."

My Grandpa Says ...

"Moses gave us Ten Commandments, Jesus reduced them down to two and self-righteous, church idiots, added 6,000 more."

My Grandpa Says ...

"If you want people to take you seriously, don't tattoo your neck or pierce your tongue."

My Grandpa Says ...

"Learn as much about as many things as possible, so that you don't sound like Britney Spears when you open your mouth."

My Grandpa Says ...

"The Jesus of the scripture razed hell, drank and made wine, was a carpenter before Home Depot and power tools, fashioned a whip and turned over the tables of religious hucksters who sold crap in the temple.

My Grandpa Says ...

"The Jesus of the scripture bashed false prophets and lying politicos and sacrificially gave up his life for us knuckleheads and then defied death and resurrected from the grave and that officially makes him the definition of a badass. He also, says, for preachers and priests, to take Jesus, the ultimate dragonslayer, and try to make him a frail, bearded lady is the sin of sins."

My Grandpa Says …

"If you demand gluten free communion at Church, then you're probably a pain in the ass in all areas of life."

My Grandpa Says ...

"He loves hunting because liberals don't hunt, and, therefore, he doesn't have to listen to their hippie garbage around the campfire."

My Grandpa Says …

"He loves hunting because he gets an ocular overload of all the beauty God has made and that beats the crap out of going to the mall."

My Grandpa Says ...

"If you hunt with your kids you won't have to hunt for them later and, by the way, hunting is a lot cheaper than rehab."

My Grandpa Says ...

"Hunting revives his primal roots and causes his senses to come alive more than staring at a computer screen ever could."

My Grandpa Says ...

"Hunters contribute more to the conservation of land and animals than PETA does by a frickin' long shot."

My Grandpa Says …

"Don't let your kids stare at iPads or drink lattes at Starbucks. Make 'em be hunters and farmers and such."

My Grandpa Says ...

"Good dads should scare their daughter's boyfriends."

My Grandpa Says ...

"You should know and understand, that our family is old school. Do not even think about approaching him with liberal, hippy, agnostic, atheistic, anti-American or tree-humping bull crap."

My Grandpa Says ...

"He was raised by country-loving, God-fearing, hard-working, meat-eating, good ole' Texan parents, and has zero tolerance for what your long-toothed, rather mannish lesbian sociology teacher at Columbia U programmed you with.
You dig?"

My Grandpa Says ...

Ladies, if your husband takes longer than you do to get ready, then you both probably need to start seeing other men.

My Grandpa Says ...

I support helping the needy, but not funding the lazy.

My Grandpa Says ...

Political correctness has become so pervasive that he can't even do a joke anymore without feminists coming over to his house and unscrewing all his light bulbs.

My Grandpa Says ...

If you want to make God
laugh, then tell
him your plans.

My Grandpa Says ...

He agrees with John Cleese when he said, 'Humor by its very nature is critical. And if you say there's a 'special' group of folks you can't offend then humor is gone and with humor goes a sense of proportion. And when that vanishes, as far as I'm concerned, you're living in 1984.'

About the Author

Doug Giles is the man behind ClashDaily.com. In addition to driving ClashDaily.com, Giles is the author of ten books including his best-sellers, "Raising Righteous and Rowdy Girls" and "Pussification: The Effeminization of the American Male."

Doug's articles have also appeared on several other print and online news sources, including Townhall.com, The Washington Times, The Daily Caller, Fox Nation, USA Today, The Wall Street Journal, The Washington Examiner, American Hunter magazine and ABC News.

Giles and his wife Margaret have two daughters: Hannah, who devastated ACORN with her 2009 nation-shaking undercover videos, and Regis who is a huntress, and owner of GirlsJustWannaHaveGuns.com

DG's interests include guns, big game hunting, big game fishing, fine art, cigars, helping wounded warriors, and being a big pain in the butt to people who dislike God and the USA.

Accolades for Giles and ClashDaily.com include

- Giles was recognized as one of "The 50 Best Conservative Columnists of 2015"
- Giles was recognized as one of "The 50 Best Conservative Columnists of 2014"
- Giles was recognized as one of "The 50 Best Conservative Columnists of 2013"
- ClashDaily.com was recognized as one of "The 100 Most Popular Conservative Websites For 2013
- Doug was noted as "Hot Conservative New Media Superman" By Politichicks

Speaking Engagements.

Doug Giles speaks to college, business, community, church, advocacy and men's groups throughout the United States and internationally. His expertise includes issues of Christianity and culture, masculinity vs. metrosexuality, big game hunting and fishing, raising righteous kids in a rank culture, the Second Amendment, personal empowerment, politics, and social change. For availability, please contact us at clash@clashdaily.com. Please use 'SPEAKING ENGAGEMENT' for your subject line when sending your request.

Other books by Doug Giles

Pussification: The Effeminization of the American Male

Raising Righteous and Rowdy Girls

Raising Boys Feminists Will Hate

Ruling in Babylon: Seven Habits of Highly Effective Twentysomethings

Political Twerps, Cultural Jerks, Church Quirks

The Bulldog Attitude: Get It or Get Left Behind

10 Habits of Decidedly Defective People: The Successful Loser's Guide to Life

A Time to Clash: Papers from a Provocative Pastor

If You're Going Through Hell, Keep Going

It has been said that daughters are God's revenge on fathers for the kind of men they were when they were young. Some would say that both Doug Giles and I, given our infamous pasts, are charter members of that club. However, Doug and I know that his two wonderful daughters and my equally wonderful daughter and two granddaughters are truly God's fantastic gift. With the wisdom of hindsight and experience Doug has written the ultimate manual for dads on raising righteous and rowdy daughters who will go out into the world well prepared- morally, physically, intellectually and with joyful hearts- to be indomitable and mighty lionesses in our cultural jungle. Through every raucous and no-holds-barred page, Doug, the incomparable Dad Drill Sergeant, puts mere men through the paces to join the ranks of the few, the proud, and the successful fathers of super daughters. The proof of Doug Giles' gold-plated credentials are Hannah and Regis Giles- two of the most fantastic, great hearted and accomplished young ladies I have ever known. This is THE BOOK that I will be giving the father of my two precious five and three year old granddaughters. Tiger Mom meet Lion Dad!

- Pat Caddell

Fox News Contributor -

PUSS-I-FI-CA-TION: The act, or process, of a man being shamed, taught, lead, pastored, drugged or otherwise coerced or cajoled into throwing out his brain, handing over his balls and formally abandoning the rarefied air of the testosterone-leader-fog that God and nature hardwired him to dwell in, and instead become a weak, effeminate, mangina sporting, shriveled up little pussy. From The Doug Giles 2016 Dictionary of Grow the Hell Up, You Pussy! In Giles' latest, and most raucous book, he takes 'Generation Pussy' from the warm wet womb of 'Pussville' to the rarefied air of 'Mantown.' This is definitely one of the most politically incorrect books to ever hit the market. It will most certainly offend the entitled whiners, but it will also be a breath of fresh air to young males who wish to be men versus hipster dandies.

It has been said that daughters are God's revenge on fathers for the kind of men they were when they were young. Some would say that both Doug Giles and I, given our infamous pasts, are charter members of that club. However, Doug and I know that his two wonderful daughters and my equally wonderful daughter and two granddaughters are truly God's fantastic gift. With the wisdom of hindsight and experience Doug has written the ultimate manual for dads on raising righteous and rowdy daughters who will go out into the world well prepared- morally, physically, intellectually and with joyful hearts- to be indomitable and mighty lionesses in our cultural jungle. Through every raucous and no-holds-barred page, Doug, the incomparable Dad Drill Sergeant, puts mere men through the paces to join the ranks of the few, the proud, and the successful fathers of super daughters. The proof of Doug Giles' gold-plated credentials are Hannah and Regis Giles- two of the most fantastic, great hearted and accomplished young ladies I have ever known. This is THE BOOK that I will be giving the father of my two precious five and three year old granddaughters. Tiger Mom meet Lion Dad!

- Pat Caddell

Fox News Contributor -

PUSS-I-FI-CA-TION: The act, or process, of a man being shamed, taught, lead, pastored, drugged or otherwise coerced or cajoled into throwing out his brain, handing over his balls and formally abandoning the rarefied air of the testosterone-leader-fog that God and nature hardwired him to dwell in, and instead become a weak, effeminate, mangina sporting, shriveled up little pussy. From The Doug Giles 2016 Dictionary of Grow the Hell Up, You Pussy! In Giles' latest, and most raucous book, he takes 'Generation Pussy' from the warm wet womb of 'Pussville' to the rarefied air of 'Mantown.' This is definitely one of the most politically incorrect books to ever hit the market. It will most certainly offend the entitled whiners, but it will also be a breath of fresh air to young males who wish to be men versus hipster dandies.

www.ingramcontent.com/pod-product-compliance
Lightning Source LLC
Chambersburg PA
CBHW072345100426
42738CB00049B/1817

www.ingramcontent.com/pod-product-compliance
Lightning Source LLC
Chambersburg PA
CBHW072345100426
42738CB00049B/1817